ᚦᛗ ᚾᚠ

THE HAVAMAL
THE SAYINGS OF THE HIGH ONE

HAIL JUSTIN
&
WELCOME
TO THE
COMMUNITY!

Topher!
2020

STUDY VERSION PRESENTED BY
THE ASATRU COMMUNITY

HÁVAMÁL

STUDY VERSION PRESENTED BY:
THE ASATRU COMMUNITY

Translation by:
The Asatru Community, Inc.

Translated by:
Vincent Panell

Cover Illustration By:
Topher W. Henry

Special thanks to:
Vincent Panell
Sage Nelson
Ivy Mulligan
And the entire Board of Directors for making this possible!

Original Icelandic text by:
Hávamál - Gestaþáttur
From the book *Eddukvæði*,
Ólafur Briem, Skálholt, 1968, Reykjavík

Included Translation by:
Olive Bray
*Hávamál - Wisdom for Wanderers
and Counsel to Guests*
The Elder or Poetic Edda,
edited and translated by Olive Bray
(London: Printed for the Viking Club, 1908),
pp. 61-111.

EDITOR'S NOTE

Our TAC Havamal was created to share with Heathen Military men, women, and veterans, all over the globe, in any military service, at no charge. It is intended to be a source of inspiration, guidance, and comfort to those Heathens fighting for their countries or with allies. It is also a study version intended for people new to Asatru, to learn the words of Odin in a simple and easy to understand translation by TAC Vice President Vincent A. Panell II.

The Havamal; Presented by The Asatru Community (Study Version) is just that. It is a study of the Havamal. As the editor of our Havamal, I took a few liberties with arranging the verses of the TAC translation done by Vincent Panell II, with his express permission, so they coincided more with the Olive Bray translation. This helps to see how the different translations can be very similar or very different, however I did not change anything in the Icelandic or the Olive Bray translations. If you look at several different translations of the Havamal you will find that not every verse is translated the same way or in the same order as another copy. If you were to put 6 different translations side by side, none of them would line up exactly identical. The Icelandic version is very difficult to read, and the words are not used the same as they are in English. Therefore, you will find discrepancies where one verse of one translation, may say something different than the same verse of another translation. There is even a "Cowboy Havamal" by Dr Jackson Crawford translated into the voice of his grandfather. Not all of his verses line up with ours either.

So, while our translation may not exactly line up with the other two translations that are in the book along side it, it is the complete poem, it is presented as a tool of learning and study. I suggest the reader also look up other translations online and learn all they can about this portion of the Codex Regius. You may also want to look up the entire Codex at some point to help you learn more about the path you have chosen to follow. My wish for everyone on this path is to learn and grow as much as you can. I wish you all the best and that you walk with the favor of the Gods!

Sincerely,
Sage R Nelson

INTRODUCTION

The Hávamál (English: /ˈhɑːvəmɑːl/ HAH-və-mahl; "sayings of the high one"; Old Norse pronunciation: [ˈhɒːwaˌmɒːl], Icelandic pronunciation: [ˈhaːvaˌmaul]) is presented as a single poem in a collection of Old Norse poems from the Viking age. The poem, itself a combination of different poems, is largely gnomic, presenting advice for living, proper conduct and wisdom to the Ancient Norseman, who due to their later highly developed practices of raiding, were called 'Vikings.' These northern European people had an oral religion which was known as Scandinavian (Germanic/Teutonic) Paganism, or more precisely; Heathenry, and the accounts of their practices as well as their traditions and mythology are only saved in a few scant manuscripts: the Prose and Poetic Edda's, the Icelandic sagas, and the Codex Regius.

The only surviving source for Hávamál is the 13th century Codex Regius and was famously translated by Henry A. Bellows in 1936. To the gnomic core of the poem, other fragments and poems dealing with wisdom and proverbs are accreted over time. A discussion of authorship or date for the individual parts would be futile, since almost every line or stanza could have been added, altered or removed at will at any time before the poem was written down in the 13th century. Individual verses or stanzas nevertheless certainly date to as early as the 10th, or even the 9th century. Thus, the line deyr fé, deyja frændr ("cattle die, kinsmen die") found in verses 76 and 77 of the Gestaþáttr can be shown to date to the 10th century, as it also occurs in the Hákonarmál by Eyvindr skáldaspillir. The part dealing with ethical conduct (the Gestaþáttr) was traditionally identified as the oldest portion of the poem by scholarship in the 19th and early 20th century. Henry Bellows (1936) identifies as the core of the poem a "collection of proverbs and wise counsels" which dates to "a very early time", but which, by the nature of oral tradition, never had a fixed form or extent. Other scholars, have identified direct influence of the Disticha Catonis on the Gestaþáttr, suggesting that also this part is a product of the high medieval period and casting doubt on the "unadulterated Germanic character" of the poem claimed by earlier commentators.

No matter the time frame of when the Hávamál was penned, or by whom, it's not a list of staunch commandments a modern-day Heathen MUST live by. It does, however, give us the backbone, if you like, of heathen social conduct that is wise advice to matters of daily living to a heathen-even today. Some of it might seem out of date, but I've never personally had an issue applying the majority of it to a modern lifestyle, and I often consult the Hávamál when I'm in two minds on something, and it rarely steers me wrong.

The verses are attributed to Odin; the implicit attribution to Odin facilitated the accretion of various mythological material also dealing with the same deity. Following the gnomic "Hávamál proper" follows the Rúnatal, an account of how Odin won the runes, and the Ljóðatal, a list of magic chants or spells.

For the most part composed in the metre Ljóðaháttr, (a metre associated with wisdom verse) Hávamál is both practical and philosophical in content. Much as the Voluspa is used by Völva's and Vitki's who practice seiðr, the Hávamál is the go-to wisdom for practitioners of Asatru everywhere.

This version you are holding in your hands was developed and printed by the volunteer members of The Asatru Community, Inc; (a.k.a. TAC) and was created to give our Heathen kindred service men and woman some comfort and guidance while away from home, protecting our country with their honorable acts of service and duty. While our country's military personal may be distanced from their homelands and Kith due to the call of duty; this copy of the Hávamál is to give them some heartfelt assurance they are revered, they are cherished, they are missed, and above all, they are Never Forgotten. -Not just by their kinsman waiting for each soldier's happy return to their hearth-fires and Frith, but also by the Asatru Community at large, who is very grateful for your service.

~May Odin watch over you, may Thor grant you strength, and may Tyr guide you in duty. Hailsa and Skal!

Ivy C Mulligan; DORA of The Asatru Community.

On the following pages, you will find:

(Center Top Text)
The Asatru Community, Inc's translation

(Left Column Text)
Original Icelandic
Text

(Right Column Text)
Olive Bray
Translation

1.

At every entry-way,
before you enter,
you should look around,
and make sure no enemy is waiting,
before setting one foot inside.

Gáttir allar
áðr gangi fram
um skoðask skyli
um skygnask skyli
því at óvíst
er at vita
hvar óvinir
sitja á fleti fyrir

At every door-way,
ere one enters,
one should spy round,
one should pry round
for uncertain is the witting
that there be no foeman sitting,
within, before one on the floor

2.

Hail, everyone!
A guest has arrived!
Where should he sit?
Tired is he that lean on
the hearth looking for
warmth and comfort.

Gefendr heilir
gestr er inn kominn
hvar skal sitja sjá?
Mjök er bráðr
sá er bröndum skal
síns um freista frama

Hail, ye Givers! a guest is come;
say! where shall he sit within?
Much pressed is he
who fain on the hearth
would seek for warmth and weal.

3.

He is in need of fire,
for he is cold through to the bone,
he seeks food and clothing
for he has traveled a far distance.

Elds er þörf
þeims inn er kominn
ok á kné kalinn
matar ok váða
es manni þörf
þeims hefir um fjall farit

He hath need of fire, who now is come,
numbed with cold to the knee;
food and clothing the wanderer craves
who has fared o'er the rimy fell.

4.

He is in need of water,
a fire to dry by,
and some companionship
with good friends.

Vats er þörf
þeims til verðar kømr
þerru ok þjóðlaðar
góðs um œðis
ef sér geta mætti
orðs ok endrþögu

He craves for water,
who comes for refreshment,
drying and friendly bidding,
marks of good will, fair fame if 'tis won,
and welcome once and again.

5.

He needs to have a
sharp mind as he travels,
for simple thought only work at home,
for only a fool sits among the wise
and knows nothing at all.

Vits er þörf
þeims viða ratar
dælt er heima hvat
at augabragði verðr
sá er ekki kann
ok með snotrum sitr

He hath need of his wits who wanders
wide, aught simple will serve at home;
but a gazing-stock is the fool who sits
mid the wise, and nothing knows.

6.

Let no man boast of his own mind,
but be cautious of what he says.
Be quiet and enter with caution into a building.
For the one that enters with caution seldom does
harm come to them.
There is no greater friend than one's own wit.

At hyggjandi sinni
skylit maðr hrœsinn vera
heldr gætinn at geði
þá er horskr ok þögull
kømr heimisgarða til
sjaldan verðr viti vörum
því at óbrigðra vin
fær maðr aldregi
en manvit mikit

Let no man glory in the greatness of his mind,
but rather keep watch o'er his wits.
Cautious and silent let him enter a dwelling;
to the heedful comes seldom harm,
for none can find a more faithful friend
than the wealth of mother wit.

7.

Let the tired traveler who seeks
drink keep quiet,
listen contently,
and look sharply,
for a wise man stays out of the way.

Hinn vari gestr
er til verðar kømr
þunnu hljóði þegir
eyrum hlýðir
en augum skoðar
svá nýsisk fróðra hverr fyrir

*Let the wary stranger who seeks refreshment
keep silent with sharpened hearing;
with his ears let him listen,
and look with his eyes;
thus each wise man spies out the way.*

8.

Happy is the person that
does for themselves,
but uneasy is a person that
relies on another.

Hinn er sæll
er sér of getr
lof ok líknstafi
ódælla er við þat
er maðr eiga skal
annars brjóstum í

*Happy is he who wins for himself
fair fame and kindly words;
but uneasy is that which a man doth own
while it lies in another's breast.*

9.

Happy is a person that has
his own knowledge in life,
for you can receive bad
information from another.

Sá er sæll
er sjalfr of á
lof ok vit meðan lifir
því at ill röð
hefr maðr opt þegit
annars brjóstum ór

*Happy is he who hath in himself
praise and wisdom in life;
for oft doth a man ill counsel get
when 'tis born in another's breast.*

10. If a person takes with him knowledge,
he can take nothing better,
for this is the greatest thing
he can take with him.

Byrði betri
berrat maðr brautu at
en sé manvit mikit
auði betra
þykkir þat í ókunnum stað
slíkt er válaðs vera

A better burden can no man bear
on the way than his mother wit;
'tis the refuge of the poor,
and richer it seems
than wealth in a world untried.

---

11. If a person takes with him knowledge,
he can take nothing better,
for a drunken mind is the worst thing
he can take with him.

Byrði betri
berrat maðr brautu at
en sé manvit mikit
vegnest verra
vegra hann velli at
an sé ofdrykkja öls

A better burden can no man bear
on the way than his mother wit:
and no worse provision can he carry with him
than too deep a draught of ale.

---

12. Alcohol is not as great a thing
as it is supposed to be,
the more you drink
the less you master yourself.

Era svá gótt
sem gótt kveða
öl alda sonum
því at færa veit
er fleira drekkr
síns til geðs gumi

Less good than they say for the sons of men
is the drinking oft of ale:
for the more they drink,
the less can they think
and keep a watch o'er their wits.

13.

The wits stealing heron
soars over gatherings,
waiting to steal men's wits,
its feathers covered me
while at Gunnlod's court.

Óminnishegri heitir
sá er yfir ölðrum þrumir
hann stelr geði guma
þess fugls fjöðrum
ek fjötraðr vask
í garði Gunnlaðar

A bird of Unmindfulness flutters
o'er ale feasts, wiling away men's wits:
with the feathers of that fowl
I was fettered once
in the garths of Gunnlos below.

14.

I was drunk beyond words
at Fjalar's banquet,
from the best party a man
will become himself soon enough.

Ölr ek varð
varð ofrölvi
at hins fróða Fjalars
því er ölðr bazt
at aptr of heimtir
hverr sitt geð gumi

Drunk was I then, I was over drunk
in that crafty Jötun's court.
But best is an ale feast when man is able
to call back his wits at once.

15.

A king's son should be bold
and thoughtful in battle,
Every man should be happy
and content till the day he dies.

Þagalt ok hugalt
skyli þjóðans barn
ok vígdjarft vera
glaðr ok reifr
skyli gumna hverr
unz sínn bíðr bana

Silent and thoughtful and bold in strife
the prince's bairn should be.
Joyous and generous let each man
show him until he shall suffer death.

16.
The foolish person thinks he will
live forever if he stays away from conflict,
but old age will not spare him
even if he stays away from battle.

Ósnjallr maðr
hyggsk munu ey lifa
ef hann við víg varask
en elli gefr
honum engi frið
þótt honum geirar gefi

A coward believes he will ever live
if he keep him safe from strife:
but old age leaves him not long in peace
though spears may spare his life.

17.
A stupid person just sits and stares,
or talks under his breath,
if he drinks
all his wit disappears.

Kópir afglapi
er til kynnis kømr
þylsk hann umbeða þrumir
alt er senn
ef hann sylg um getr
uppi er þá geð guma

A fool will gape when he goes to a friend,
and mumble only, or mope;
but pass him the ale cup
and all in a moment
the mind of that man is shown.

18.
A person must travel
the world many times,
before he is wise enough
to see the workings of others.

Sá einn veit
er víða ratar
ok hefr fjölð um farit
hverju geði
stýrir gumna hverr
sá er vitandi er vits

He knows alone who has wandered wide,
and far has fared on the way,
what manner of mind a man doth own
who is wise of head and heart.

19.

Only drink your share and
speak useful words or do not speak at all,
no one can blame you for bad manners,
if you retire to bed early.

Haldit maðr á keri
drekki þó at hófi mjöð
mæli þarft eða þegi
ókynnis þess
var þik engi maðr
at þú gangir snemma at sofa

Keep not the mead cup
but drink thy measure;
speak needful words or none:
none shall upbraid thee
for lack of breeding
if soon thou seek' st thy rest.

20.

A greedy person eats until
he makes himself sick,
if he sits with those that are wise,
they will just make fun of him.

Gröðugr halr
nema geðs viti
etr sér aldrtrega
opt fær hlœgis
er með horskum kømr
manni heimskum magi

A greedy man, if he be not mindful,
eats to his own life's hurt:
oft the belly of the fool will bring him
to scorn when he seeks the circle of the wise.

21.

The herds know when they
have stayed long enough,
the foolish will over stay their welcome.

Hjarðir þat vitu
nær þær heim skulu
ok ganga þá af grasi
en ósviðr maðr
kann ævagi
síns um mál maga

Herds know the hour of their going home
and turn them again from the grass;
but never is found a foolish man
who knows the measure of his maw.

22.

An evil small-minded person
will only see flaws in everything,
not seeing his own flaws.

Vesall maðr
ok illa skapi
hlær at hvívetna
hitki hann veit
er hann vita þyrpti
at hann era vamma vanr

The miserable man and evil minded
makes of all things mockery,
and knows not
that which he best should know,
that he is not free from faults.

23.

A stupid person will lay awake at night
thinking of all their problems,
they are tired when morning comes,
and their problems still exist.

Ósviðr maðr
vakir um allar nætr
ok hyggr at hvívetna
þá er móðr
er at morni kømr
alt er vil sem var

The unwise man is awake all night,
and ponders everything over;
when morning comes
he is weary in mind,
and all is a burden as ever.

24.

A foolish person thinks that all who
laugh with them are friends,
if others mock them behind their backs,
they will never know.

Ósnotr maðr
hyggr sér alla vera
viðhlæjendr vini
hitki hann fiðr
þótt þeir um hann fár lesi
ef hann með snotrum sitr

The unwise man weens all who smile
and flatter him are his friends,
nor notes how oft they speak him ill
when he sits in the circle of the wise.

25.

A foolish person thinks that
all that laugh with them are friends,
but he will see who his friends are
when he goes to court.

Ósnotr maðr
hyggr sér alla vera
viðhlæjendr vini
þá þat fiðr
er at þingi kømr
at hann á formælendr fá

The unwise man weens all who smile
and flatter him are his friends;
but when he shall come into court
he shall find there are few to defend his cause.

26.

A stupid person thinks he knows all,
but when asked about certain things,
it will be discovered they know little.

Ósnotr maðr
þykkisk alt vita
ef hann á sér í vá veru
hitki hann veit
hvat hann skal við kveða
ef hans freista firar

The unwise man thinks all to know,
while he sits in a sheltered nook;
but he knows not one thing,
what he shall answer,
if men shall put him to proof.

27.

A stupid person should not
talk when with a group,
the less they talk,
no one will notice they know nothing.
(And if they talk to like-minded people it is safe)

Ósnotr maðr
er með aldir kømr
þat er bazt at hann þegi
engi þat veit
at hann ekki kann
name hann mæli til mart
veita maðr
hinn er vætki veit
þótt hann mæli til mart

For the unwise man 'tis best to be mute
when he come amid the crowd,
for none is aware of his lack of wit
if he wastes not too many words;
for he who lacks wit shall never learn
though his words flow ne'er so fast.

28.

A smart person will ask questions
and answer them as well,
no one can keep something from getting out,
once it is spoken to others.

Fróðr sá þykkisk
er fregna kann
ok segja hit sama
eyvitu leyna
megu ýta synir
því er gengr of guma

Wise, he is deemed who can question well,
and also answer back:
the sons of men can no secret make
of the tidings told in their midst.

29.

A person that talks and never listens,
is bound to mess up,
a ready tongue if not controlled,
will cause you harm.

Œrna mælir
sá er eva þegir
staðlausu stafi
hraðmælt tunga
nema haldendr eigi
opt sér ógótt um gelr

Too many unstable words are spoken
by him who ne'er holds his peace;
the hasty tongue sings its own mishap
if it be not bridled in.

30.

Take time to make your judgment
of someone that visits,
many seem smart when they are silent
and not talked to.

At augabragði
skala maðr anna hafa
þótt til kynnis komi
margr þá fróðr þykkisk
ef hann freginn erat
ok nái hann þurrfjallr þruma

Let no man be held as a laughing-stock,
though he come as guest for a meal:
wise enough seem many while they sit
dry-skinned and are not put to proof.

31.

A person is wise to stay away from
those that pick on others,
they may sit and talk to what
they think are friends,
only to find out they are the foes.

Fróðr þykkisk
sá er flótta tekr
gestr at gest hæðinn
veita görla
sá er of verði glissir
þótt hann með grömum glami

A guest thinks him witty
who mocks at a guest and runs
from his wrath away;
but none can be sure who jests at a meal
that he makes not fun among foes.

32.

Even friends will fight during gatherings,
nothing can stop it.

Gunnar margir
erusk gagnhollir
en at virði vrekask
aldar róg
þat mun æ vera
órir gestr við gest

Oft, though their hearts lean towards
one another, friends are divided at table;
ever the source of strife 'twill be,
that guest will anger guest.

33.

A person should eat well,
before visiting friends,
or they will sit around starved
and speak few words.

Árliga verðar
skyli maðr opt fá
nema til kynnis komi
sitr ok snópir
lætr sem solginn sé
ok kann fregna at fá

A man should take always his meals
betimes unless he visit a friend,
or he sits and mopes,
and half famished seems,
and can ask or answer nought.

34.

An untrue friend lives far away
even though he is near,
a true friend will travel many miles to visit.

Afhvart mikit
er til ills vinar
þótt á brautu búi
en til góðs vinar
liggja gagnvegir
þótt hann sé firr farinn

Long is the round to a false friend leading,
e'en if he dwell on the way:
but though far off fared,
to a faithful friend
straight are the roads and short.

35.

Do not overstay your welcome
when visiting,
love turns to discontent
when you stay too long.

Ganga skal
skala gestr vera
ey í einum stað
ljúfr verðr leiðr
ef lengi sitr
annars fletjum á

A guest must depart again on his way,
nor stay in the same place ever;
if he bide too long on another's bench
the loved one soon becomes loathed.

36.

Be content with your life
and what you have,
even if it is little,
it is far better than begging.

Bú er betra
þótt lítit sé
halr er heima hverr
þótt tvær geitr
eigi ok taugreptan sal
þat er þó betra an bœn

One's own house is best,
though small it may be;
each man is master at home;
though he have but two goats
and a bark-thatched hut
'tis better than craving a boon.

37.

Be content with your life
and what you have,
a person's spirit is destroyed
when they have to beg.

Bú er betra
þótt lítit sé
halr er heima hverr
blóðugt er hjarta
þeims biðja skal
sér í mál hvert matar

One's own house is best,
though small it may be,
each man is master at home;
with a bleeding heart will he beg,
who must, his meat at every meal.

38.

Never leave your weapons behind,
for you may never know
when you need them.

Vápnum sínum
skala maðr velli á
feti ganga framar
því at óvist er at vita
nær verðr á vegum úti
geirs um þörf guma

Let a man never stir on his road a step
without his weapons of war;
for unsure is the knowing
when need shall arise
of a spear on the way without.

39.

I have never met a person that
would not receive a gift,
or one so happy with what they had,
they did not care if money was made.

Fanka ek mildan mann
eða svá matar góðan
at værit þiggja þegit
eða síns féar
svá gjöflan
at leið sé laun ef þiggr

I found none so noble or free with his food,
who was not gladdened with a gift,
nor one who gave of his gifts such store
but he loved reward, could he win it.

40.

A person should spend their money
on what they want,
saving it for others may not help them,
things do not always work out the way we want.

Féar síns
er fengit hefir
skylit maðr þörf þola
opt sparir leiðum
þats hefir ljúfum hugat
mart gengr verr en varir

Let no man stint him and suffer need
of the wealth he has won in life;
oft is saved for a foe
what was meant for a friend,
and much goes worse than one weens.

41.

Give gifts to friends,
for they are happy to receive them,
giving to each other makes friendships last,
as long as the giving is equal on all sides.

Vápnum ok váðum
skulu vinir gleðjask
þat er á sjalfum sýnst
viðr gefendr ok endrgefendr
erusk vinir lengst,
ef þat bíðr at verða vel

With raiment and arms shall friends
gladden each other,
so has one proved oneself;
for friends last longest, if fate be fair
who give and give again.

42.

A person keep faith with all
their friends always returning
gift or favor for gift or favor,
happiness should be rewarded
with happiness and deceit with deceit.

Vin sínum
skal maðr vinr vera
ok gjalda gjöf við gjöf
hlátr við hlátri
skyli hölðar taka
en lausung við lygi

To his friend a man should bear him
as friend, and gift for gift bestow,
laughter for laughter let him exchange,
but leasing pay for a lie.

43.

A person should be faithful
to their friends and their friends,
it is not wise to make friends
with your friends' enemies.

Vin sínum
skal maðr vinr vera
þeim ok þess vinr
en óvinar síns
skyli engi maðr
vinar vinr vera

To his friend a man should bear him as
friend, to him and a friend of his;
but let him beware that he be not the friend
of one who is friend to his foe.

44.

If you have a friend you trust,
and want to do them right,
open up to them, give them gifts,
and visit them often.

Veiztu ef þú vin átt
þanns þú vel trúir
ok vill þú af honum gótt geta
geði skalt við þann
blanda ok gjöfum skipta
fara at finna opt

Hast thou a friend whom thou trustest well,
from whom thou cravest good?
Share thy mind with him,
gifts exchange with him, fare to find him oft.

45.

If you do not trust someone and
want them to do you right,
let your voice be true but
not your thought,
pay back deceit with deceit.

Ef þú át annan
þanns þú illa trúir
vildu af honum þó gótt geta
fagrt skalt við þann mæla
en flátt hyggja
ok gjalda lausung við lygi

But hast thou one whom thou trustest ill
yet from whom thou cravest good?
Thou shalt speak him fair, but falsely think,
and leasing pay for a lie.

46.

Here is more advice for
someone you distrust,
laugh when they do,
conceal your true intentions,
give gift for gift.

Þat er enn of þann
er þú illa trúir
ok þér er grunr at hans geði
hlæja skaltu við þeim
ok um hug mæla
glík skulu gjöld gjöfum

Yet further of him whom thou trusted ill,
and whose mind thou dost misdoubt;
thou shalt laugh with him
but withhold thy thought,
for gift with like gift should be paid.

47.

As a young man I traveled by myself,
and would get lost,
I felt richest when I made a new friend,
no one that is alone is happy.

Ungr var ek forðum
fór ek einn saman
þá varð ek villr vega
auðigr þóttumk
er ek annan fann
maðr er manns gaman

Young was I once, I walked alone,
and bewildered seemed in the way;
then I found me another and rich
I thought me, for man is the joy of man.

48.

Brave and generous people
have the best lives,
and are seldom unhappy,
those that are afraid of everything
are fools and live unhappy lives.

Mildir fræknir
menn bazt lifa
sjaldan sút ala
en ósnjallr maðr
uggir hotvetna
sýtir æ gløggr við gjöfum

Most blest is he who lives free and bold
and nurses never a grief,
for the fearful man is dismayed by aught,
and the mean one mourns over giving.

49.

When I saw two scarecrows,
I dressed them in my clothes,
they looked like warriors,
no one seeks a naked hero.

Váðir mínar
gaf ek velli at
tveim trémönnum
rekkar þat þóttusk
er þeir ript höfðu
neiss er nøkkviðr halr

My garments once I gave in the field
to two land-marks made as men;
heroes they seemed when once they were clothed;
'tis the naked who suffer shame!

50.

A pine tree dies in a clearing,
its bark and needle cannot save it.
How can a person hated by all,
live for long.

Hrørnar þöll
sú er stendr þorpi á
hlýrat henni börkr né barr
svá er maðr
sá er mangi ann
hvat skal hann lengi lifa?

The pine tree wastes which is perched on the hill,
nor bark nor needles shelter it;
such is the man whom none doth love;
for what should he longer live?

51.

Hotter than friendship five
days among false friends,
then on the six day comes around,
it dies down and all love
between you is lost.

Eldi heitari
brinn með illum vinum
friðr fimm daga,
en þá sloknar
es hinn sétti kømr
ok versnar allr vinskapr

Fiercer than fire among ill friends
for five days love will burn;
bun anon 'tis quenched,
when the sixth day comes,
and all friendship soon is spoiled.

52.
You do not always have to give large gifts,
small ones work just as well,
food and a raised drink
have made many friends.

Mikit eitt
skala manni gefa
opt kaupir sér í lítlu lof
með hálfum hleifi
ok með höllu keri
fekk ek mér félaga

Not great things alone must one give to another,
praise oft is earned for nought;
with half a loaf and a tilted bowl
I have found me many a friend.

53.
There are small shores and seas,
and people with little sense,
not all are equal in wisdom,
there is no shortness of
small-minded people.

Lítilla sanda
lítilla sæva
lítil eru geð guma
því at allir menn
urðut jafnspakir
hálf er öld hvar

Little the sand if little the seas,
little are minds of men,
for ne'er in the world were all equally wise,
'tis shared by the fools and the sage

54.
A person should be wise
but not seek out too much wisdom,
those that live the best lives
do not know too much.

Meðalsnotr
skyli manna hverr
æva til snotr sé
þeim er fyrða
fegrst at lifa
er vel mart vitut

Wise in measure let each man be;
but let him not wax too wise;
for never the happiest of men is he
who knows much of many things.

55.

A person should be wise
but not seek too much wisdom,
a man is seldom happy
if he knows too much.

Meðalsnotr
skyli manna hverr
æva til snotr sé
því at snotrs manns hjarta
verðr sjaldan glatt,
ef sá er alsnotr er á

Wise in measure should each man be;
but let him not wax too wise;
seldom a heart will sing with joy
if the owner be all too wise.

56.

A person should be wise
but not seek too much wisdom,
if you do not look too far ahead,
you can truly live free from worry.

Meðalsnotr
skyli manna hverr
æva til snotr sé
ørlög sín
viti engi fyrir
þeim er sorgalausastr sefi

Wise in measure should each man be,
but ne'er let him wax too wise:
who looks not forward to learn his fate
unburdened heart will bear.

57.

Flames jump from log to log,
fire makes fire.
A man's wisdom shows when he talks,
stupidity makes no sound.

Brandr af brandi
brinn unz brunninn er
funi kveykisk af funa
maðr af manni
verðr at máli kuðr
en til dœlskr af dul

Brand kindles from brand until it be burned,
spark is kindled from spark,
man unfolds him by speech with man,
but grows over secret through silence.

58.

Rise early if you seek another
man's lifestyle and wealth,
a sleeping wolf seldom kills on a hunt,
nor will a warrior win a battle
while lying down.

Ár skal rísa
sá er annars vill
fé eða fjör hafa
sjaldan liggjandi úlfr
lær um getr
né sofandi maðr sigr

He must rise betimes who fain of another
or life or wealth would win;
scarce falls the prey to sleeping wolves,
or to slumberers victory in strife.

59.

Rise early if you have
few people to help you,
and do your own work,
wealth slips by when you lay in bed,
the work is half the wealth you have.

Ár skal rísa
sá er á yrkendr fá
ok ganga síns verka á vit
mart um dvelr
þann er um morgin sefr
hálfr er auðr und hvötum

He must rise betimes who hath few
to serve him, and see to his work himself;
who sleeps at morning is hindered much,
to the keen is wealth half-won.

60.

A person can measure his roof and house,
as well as how much wood is needed
to fuel his fire for the winter.

Þurra skíða
ok þakinna næfra
þess kann maðr mjöt
ok þess viðar
er vinnask megi
mál ok misseri

Of dry logs saved and roof-bark stored
a man can know the measure,
of fire-wood too which should last him
out quarter and half years to come.

61.

Be hungry when you ride to the Thing,
be sure your clothes are clean,
you will not be judged
by your clothes or your horse,
even though he is not a true prize.

Þveginn ok mettr
ríði maðr þingi at
þótt hann sét væddr til vel
skúa ok bróka
skammisk engi maðr
né hests in heldr
þótt hann hafit góðan

Fed and washed should one ride to court
though in garments none too new;
thou shalt not shame thee for shoes or breeks,
nor yet for a sorry steed.

62.

Soaring over the sea,
the eagle watches over it all,
he is fond of the person
that travels but has few friends.

Snapir ok gnapir
er til sævar kømr
örn á aldinn mar
svá er maðr
er með mörgum kømr
ok á formælendr fá

Like an eagle swooping over old ocean,
snatching after his prey,
so comes a man into court
who finds there are few to defend his cause.

63.

A wise person will ask and answer questions,
one can know something but not two,
everyone knows if more than two do.

Fregna ok segja
skal fróðra hverr
sá er vill heitinn horskr
einn vita
né annarr skal
þjóð veit ef þrír ro

Each man who is wise and would wise
be called must ask and answer aright.
Let one know thy secret,
but never a second,
if three a thousand shall know.

64. A clever person will not show all their strength,
for they discover that when with others
no one claims all the courage.

Ríki sitt
skyli ráðsnotra
hverr í hófi hafa
þá hann þat finnr
er með frœknum kømr
at engi er einna hvatastr

A wise counselled man will be mild in bearing
and use his might in measure,
lest when he come his fierce foes among
he find others fiercer than he.

---

65. Often for the words spoken to others,
a person receives their rewards.

Orða þeira
er maðr öðrum segir
opt hann gjöld um getr

Each man should be watchful
and wary in speech,
and slow to put faith in a friend.
for the words which one to another speaks
he may win reward of ill.

---

66. To many times I came to early or too late,
the mead was gone or had not been brewed,
those that are unwelcome will find no feasts.

Mikilsti snemma
kom ek í marga staði
en til síð í suma
öl var drukkit
sumt var ólagat
sjaldan hittir leiðr í lið

At many a feast I was far too late,
and much too soon at some;
drunk was the ale or yet unserved:
never hits he the joint who is hated.

67.
At some gatherings I was treated well,
when I did not ask to eat,
or if there was more than enough and I ate.

Hér ok hvar
myndi mér heim of boðit
ef þyrftak at málungi mat
eða tvau lær hengi
at ins tryggva vinar
þars ek hafða eitt etit

Here and there to a home I had haply been asked
had I needed no meat at my meals,
or were two hams left hanging in the house
of that friend where I had partaken of one.

68.
For people the greatest things
are fire, the sun, great health,
and living a great life.

Eldr er beztr
með ýta sonum
ok sólar sýn
heilyndi sitt
ef maðr hafa náir
án við löst at lifa

Most dear is fire to the sons of men,
most sweet the sight of the sun;
good is health if one can but keep it,
and to live a life without shame.

69.
Even if a person falls ill
they can still be happy,
they can rejoice in their children,
their friends, their wealth,
and the work they have done in their life.

Erat maðr alls vesall
þótt hann sé illa heill
sumr er af sonum sæll
sumr af frændum
sumr af fé œrnu
sumr af verkum vel

Not reft of all is he who is ill,
for some are blest in their bairns,
some in their kin and some in their wealth,
and some in working well.

70.

It is better to live your life,
than to not live at all.
While the wealthy stay warm by their fire,
the dead lay outside cold.

Betra er lifðum
en sé ólifðum
ey getr kvikr kú
eld sá ek upp brenna
auðgum manni fyrir
en úti var dauðr fyr durum

More blest are the living than the lifeless,
'tis the living who come by the cow;
I saw the hearth-fire burn in the rich man's hall
and himself lying dead at the door.

71.

The lame ride upon horses,
the hand-less drive the herds,
the deaf may do great in battle,
better to not see them burned on a pyre,
dead men cannot do anything.

Haltr ríðr hrossi
hjörð rekr handarvanr
daufr vegr ok dugir
blindr er betri
en brenndr sé
nýtr manngi nás

The lame can ride horse,
the handless drive cattle,
the deaf one can fight and prevail,
'tis happier for the blind
than for him on the bale-fire,
but no man hath care for a corpse.

72.

Though he is born when you are dead,
it is better to have a son,
you only see tombstones
for those with kinsman.

Sonr er betri
þótt sé síð of alinn
eptir genginn guma
sjaldan bautarsteinar
standa brautu nær
nema reisi niðr at nið

Best have a son though he be late born
and before him the father be dead:
seldom are stones on the wayside raised
save by kinsmen to kinsmen.

73.

Two things cause trouble for a man.
His tongue and the fur coat
that covers his hands.
The darkness is your friend
if you have enough food.
A ship has many small cabins.
Do not trust the Autumn night.
The weather may stay
the same for five days,
but changes many times in a month.

Tveir ro eins herjar
tunga er höfuðs bani
er mér í heðin hvern
handar væni

Two are hosts against one
the tongue is the head's bane,
'neath a rough hide a hand may be hid;
he is glad at nightfall who knows of his lodging,
short is the ship's berth,
and changeful the autumn night,
much veers the wind ere the fifth day
and blows round yet more in a month.

74.

He who knows nothing
does not know this,
money controls men,
one that has it,
and another that wants it,
do either of them not have
a need for complaint.

Nótt verðr feginn
sá er nesti trúir
skammar ro skips rár
hverf er haustgríma
fjölð um viðrir
á fimm dögum
en meira á mánuði

He that learns nought will never know
how one is the fool of another,
for if one be rich another is poor
and for that should bear no blame.

75.

Livestock dies, family dies,
you will die yourself,
but words of praise
about you will not,
when a man has fame.

Veita hinn
er vættki veit
margr verðr af aurum api
maðr er auðigr
annarr óauðigr
skylit þann vítka vár

Cattle die and kinsmen die,
thyself too soon must die,
but one thing never, I ween, will die,
fair fame of one who has earned.

76.

Livestock dies, family dies,
you will die yourself,
one thing that will never die
is a man's reputation.

Deyr fé
deyja frændr
deyr sjálfr it sama
en orðstírr
deyr aldregi
hveim er sér góðan getr

Cattle die and kinsmen die,
thyself too soon must die,
but one thing never, I ween, will die,
the doom on each one dead.

77.

I saw the full fields of Fitjung's sons,
who are now poor.
Do not trust your wealth,
for it can be gone in a blink of the eye.

Deyr fé
deyja frændr
deyr sjálfr it sama
ek veit einn
at aldri deyr
dómr um dauðan hvern

Full-stocked folds had the Fatling's sons,
who bear now a beggar's staff:
brief is wealth, as the winking of an eye,
most faithless ever of friends.

78.

When a person is not wise,
they only have to win livestock
or another person's caress,
their self-esteem soars,
while their wits do not,
they are swollen with self-pride.

Fullar grindr
sá ek fyr Fitjungs sonum
nú bera þeir vánarvöl
svá er auðr
sem augabragð
hann er valtastr vina

If haply a fool should find for himself
wealth or a woman's love,
pride waxes in him but wisdom never
and onward he fares in his folly.

79.

Those who read the runes
set down by Odin
and stained by the Sage,
will not waste words.

Ósnotr maðr
ef eignask getr
fé eða fljóðs munuð
metnaðr honum þróask
en mannvit aldregi
fram gengr hann drjúgt í dul

All will prove true that thou askest of runes,
those that are come from the gods,
which the high Powers wrought,
and which Odin painted:
then silence is surely best.

80.

Give praise to the day at night,
a woman that has died,
a sword proven to in battle,
a maiden married,
ice you have been across,
and mead you have savored.

Þat er þá reynt
er þú at rúnum spyrr
inum reginkunnum
þeim er gerðu ginnregin
ok fáði fimbulþulr
þá hefir hann bazt ef hann þegir

Praise day at even, a wife when dead,
a weapon when tried,
a maid when married,
ice when 'tis crossed,
and ale when 'tis drunk.

81. Cut the trees when the wind is blowing,
only sail when weather is fair,
talk to maidens when it becomes dark;
for there are many eyes looking
during the day.
Ask for speed of the ship,
protection from your shield,
strength in the sword,
and a kiss from a maiden.

At kveldi skal dag leyfa
konu er brennd er
mæki er reyndr er
mey er gefin er
ís er yfir kømr
öl er drukkit er

Hew wood in wind, sail the seas in a breeze,
woo a maid in the dark,
for day's eyes are many,
work a ship for its gliding,
a shield for its shelter, a sword for its striking,
a maid for her kiss.

---

82. Drink mead by the fire,
skate on the ice,
buy fit horses and
battle tested swords,
fatten horses in the barn
and dogs in your home.

Í vindi skal við höggva
veðri á sjó róa
myrkri við man spjalla
mörg eru dags augu
á skip skal skriðar orka
en á skjöld til hlífar
mæki höggs
en mey til kossa

Drink ale by the fire, but slide on the ice;
buy a steed when 'tis lanky,
a sword when 'tis rusty;
feed thy horse neath a roof,
and thy hound in the yard.

83.

Never trust the words of a maiden,
or count her to be constant,
their hearts can turn in a minute,
their minds are made to change.

Við eld skal öl drekka
en á ísi skríða
magran mar kaupa
en mæki saurgan
heima hest feita
en hund á búi

The speech of a maiden should no man trust
nor the words which a woman says;
for their hearts were shaped
on a whirling wheel
and falsehood fixed in their breasts.

84.

A bow creaking,
a fire burning bright,
a howling wolf,
a crow cawing,
a pig squealing,
a tree without roots,
smoke rising,
a pot boiling,

Meyjar orðum
skyli manngi trúa
né því er kveðr kona
því at á hverfanda hvéli
váru þeim hjörtu sköpuð
brigð í brjóst um lagit

Breaking bow, or flaring flame,
ravening wolf, or croaking raven,
routing swine, or rootless tree,
waxing wave, or seething cauldron,

85.

A dart flying,
waves falling,
fresh ice,
a coiled snake,
a bride's pillow talk,
a sword broken,
a bear playing
or a king's son,

Brestanda boga
brennanda loga
gínanda úlfi
galandi kráku
rýtanda svíni
rótlausum viði
vaxanda vági
vellanda katli

Flying arrows, or falling billow,
ice of a nighttime, coiling adder,
woman's bed-talk, or broken blade,
play of bears or a prince's child,

86.

A sick cow,
a willing slave,
sweet words from a volva,
the newly dead,

Fljúganda fleini
fallandi báru
ísi einnættum
ormi hringlegnum
brúðar beðmálum
eða brotnu sverði
bjarnar leiki
eða barni konungs

Sickly calf or self-willed thrall,
witch's flattery, new-slain foe,
brother's slayer, though seen on the highway,
half burned house, or horse too swift,
be never so trustful as these to trust.

87.

Your kin's murderer met on the path,
a burned house,
or a horse that is too fast,
a person is too trusting,
if they take a chance on these.

Sjúkum kálfi
sjálfráða þræli
völu vilmæli
val nýfeldum

Let none put faith in the first sown fruit
nor yet in his son too soon;
whim rules the child,
and weather the field, each is open to chance.

88.

Never trust a field
that is planted too early,
or a son too young,
weather controls crops,
a son grows with wisdom,
you run a risk with both.

Akri ársánum
trúi engi maðr
né til snemma syni
veðr ræðr akri
en vit syni
hætt er þeira hvárt

Like the love of women whose thoughts are lies,
is the driving un-roughshod o'er slippery ice
of a two-year-old, ill-tamed and gay;
or in a wild wind steering a helmless ship,
or the lame catching reindeer
in the rime-thawed fell.

89.

You will find the love,
of an unfaithful woman like this:
a shoed horse on ice,
a young untrained two-year-old,
a ship with no rudder in a storm,
or a lame man running on an icy hill.

Bróðurbana sínum
þótt á brautu mœti
húsi hálfbrunnu
hesti alskjótum
þá er jór ónýtr
ef einn fótr brotnar
verðit maðr svá tryggr
at þessu trúi öllu

Now plainly I speak, since both I have seen;
unfaithful is man to maid;
we speak them fairest when thoughts
are falsest and wile the wisest of hearts.

90.

Believe me - I know both -
men do not stay faithful to women,
we speak fairly,
when we think falsely,
to fool the wise.

Svá er friðr kvenna
þeira er flátt hyggja
sem aki jó óbryddum
á ísi hálum
teitum tvévetrum
ok sé tamr illa
eða í byr óðum
beiti stjórnlausu
eða skyli haltr henda
hrein í þáfjalli

Let him speak soft words and offer wealth
who longs for a woman's love,
praise the shape of the shining maid
he wins who thus doth woo.

91.
Speak loving words and give gifts,
when trying to win a woman's love,
flatter her by complimenting her looks,
praise will get you the prize.

Bert ek nú mæli
því at ek bæði veit
brigðr er karla hugr konum
þá vér fegrst mælum
er vér flást hyggjum
þat tælir horska hugi

Never a whit should one blame another
whom love hath brought into bonds:
oft a witching form will fetch the wise
which holds not the heart of fools.

92.
Do not let a man mock another,
laughing about his love,
the dumb may be safe,
when the wise give way to their own folly.

Fagrt skal mæla
ok fé bjóða
sá er vill fljóðs ást fá
líki leyfa
ins ljósa mans
sá fær er fríar

Never a whit should one blame another
for a folly which many befalls;
the might of love makes sons of men
into fools who once were wise.

93.
Do not let a man mock another
for what others suffer from,
for wise men can be made fools by love.

Ástar firna
skyli engi maðr
annan aldregi
opt fá á horskan
er á heimskan ne fá
lostfagrir litir

The mind knows alone what is nearest the heart
and sees where the soul is turned:
no sickness seems to the wise
so sore as in nought to know content.

94.
Only you know what lives in your heart,
look clearly into yourself,
for the wise there is no greater sickness,
as having nothing left to love.

Eyvitar firna
er maðr annan skal
þess er um margan gengr guma
heimska ór horskum
gørir hölða sonu
sá inn mátki munr

This once I felt when I sat without
in the reeds, and looked for my love;
body and soul of me was that sweet maiden
yet never I won her as wife.

95.
I realized while waiting for that fair woman,
that I loved her beyond her body and soul,
but I had not my desire.

Hugr einn þat veit
er býr hjarta nær
einn er hann sér um sefa
øng er sótt verri
hveim snotrum manni
en sér øngu at una

Billing's daughter I found on her bed,
fairer than sunlight sleeping,
and the sweets of lordship seemed to me nought,
save I lived with that lovely form.

96.
I saw Billing's daughter
laying in her bed sleeping,
then the earth seemed
without happiness,
unless I could lay beside her.

Þat ek þá reynda
er ek í reyri sat
ok vættak míns munar
hold ok hjarta
var mér in horska mær
þeygi ek hana at heldr hefik

"Yet nearer evening come thou, Odin,
if thou wilt woo a maiden:
all were undone save two knew alone
such a secret deed of shame."

97.

"You must wait, Odin;
when it gets dark,
come back if you want to court me."
It is unlucky if others
witnessed my weakness.

Billings mey
ek fann beðjum á
sólhvíta sofa
jarls ynði
þótti mér ekki vera
nema við þat lík at lifa

So away I turned from my wise intent,
and deemed my joy assured,
for all her liking and all her love
I weened that I yet should win.

98.

So, I returned,
wanting to receive my desire,
being sure that at last,
what I longed for,
would be granted by her.

Auk nær apni
skaltu Óðinn koma
ef þú vilt þér mæla man
alt eru ósköp
nema einir viti
slíkan löst saman

When I came ere long the war troop bold
were watching and waking all:
with burning brands and torches borne
they showed me my sorrowful way.

99.

All for nothing that night,
she fought like a warrior barring the way,
she had lead me on a great chase.

Aptr ek hvarf
ok unna þóttumk
vísum vilja frá
hitt ek hugða
at ek hafa mynda
geð hennar alt ok gaman

Yet nearer morning I went, once more,
the housefolk slept in the hall,
but soon I found a barking dog
tied fast to that fair maid's couch.

100. When the sun came up and I returned,
no one was moving around,
the only thing I saw was the
wretched dog that woman had tied to the bed.

Svá kom ek næst
at in nýta var
vígdrótt öll um vakin
með brennandum ljósum
ok bornum viði
svá var mér vílstígr of vitaðr

Many a sweet maid when one knows
her mind is fickle found towards men:
I proved it well when that prudent lass
I sought to lead astray:
shrewd maid, she sought me with every insult
and I won therewith no wife.

---

101. Let there be no mistake,
there are many women fickle and false,
I learned this the hard way
when I tried to lure one to love;
she made me suffer many times
and gave me no delight.

Ok nær morni
er ek var enn um kominn
þá var saldrótt um sofin
grey eitt ek þá fann
innar góðu konu
bundit beðjum á

In thy home be joyous and generous to guests
discreet shalt thou be in thy bearing,
mindful and talkative,
wouldst thou gain wisdom,
oft making me mention of good.
He is "Simpleton" named who has nought to say,
for such is the fashion of fools.

102.

Be happy at home with guest,
but you must have a mind.
Knowing a lot and talking much,
he will be known to be wise,
a fool never says anything
because he is not very smart.

Mörg er góð mær
ef görva kannar
hugbrigð við hali
þá ek þat reynda
er it ráðspaka
teygða ek á flærðir fljóð
háðungar hverrar
leitaði mér it horska man
ok hafða ek þess vættki vífs

I sought that old Jötun, now safe am I back,
little served my silence there;
but whispering many soft speeches I won
my desire in Suttung's halls.

103.

I looked for the old giant,
silence would not do,
so, I spoke many words.
My errand would have failed,
had I been silent in Suttung's hall.

Heima glaðr gumi
ok við gesti reifr
sviðr skal um sik vera
minnigr ok málugr
ef hann vill margfróðr vera
opt skal góðs geta
fimbulfambi heitir
sá er fátt kann segja
þat er ósnotrs aðal

I bored me a road there with Rati's tusk
and made room to pass through the rock;
while the ways of the Jötuns
stretched over and under,
I dared my life for a draught.

104.   I cut my path through the rock,
a perilous journey up the path to the giant.

Inn aldna jötum ek sótta
nú em ek aptr um kominn
fátt gat ek þegjandi þar
mörgum orðum
mælta ek í minn frama
í Suttungs sölum

'Twas Gunnlod who gave me on a golden throne,
a draught of the glorious mead,
but with poor reward did I pay her back
for her true and troubled heart.

---

105.   From her throne, Gunnlod gave me
a horn of great mead. An ill reward she
was given in return for her kindness,
for her heavy heart.

Gunnlöð mér um gaf
gullnum stóli á
drykk ins dýra mjaðar
ill iðgjöld
lét ek hana eptir hafa
síns ins heila hugar
síns ins svára sefa

In a wily disguise I worked my will;
little is lacking to the wise,
for the Soul-stirrer now, sweet Mead of Song,
is brought to men's earthly abode.

---

106.   From that bargain I was given a lot,
now I have great wisdom,
the magic mead of poetry,
left with the Aesir.

Rata munn
létumk rúms um fá
ok um grjót gnaga
yfir ok undir
stóðumk jötna vegir
svá hætta ek höfði til

I misdoubt me if ever again I had come
from the realms of the Jötun race,
had I not served me of Gunnlod,
sweet woman, her whom I held in mine arms.

107. I don't think I would have made it back,
if it were not for Gunnlod,
the woman who laid in my arms.

Vel keypts litar
hefi ek vel notit
fás er fróðum vant
því at Óðrerir
er nú upp kominn
á alda vés jarðar

Came forth, next day, the dread Frost Giants,
and entered the High One's Hall:
they asked, was the Baleworker back mid the Powers,
or had Suttung slain him below?

---

108. The next day the frost giants
found the High One and asked
if Odin was with the Aesir or
if he had been killed.

Ifi er mér á
at ek væra enn kominn
jötna görðum ór
ef ek Gunnlaðar ne nytak
innar góðu konu
þeirar er lögðumk arm yfir

A ring-oath Odin I trow had taken
how shall one trust his troth?
'twas he who stole the mead from Suttung,
and Gunnlod caused to weep.

---

109. "Odin did not honor his oath
that was sworn on the ring,
what good is any oath he makes?
He stole the mead from the feast of Sutting's
and Gunnlod is grieving".

Ins hindra dags
gengu hrímþursar
Háva ráðs at fregna
Háva höllu í
at Bölverki þeir spurðu
ef hann væri með böndum kominn
eða hefði honum Suttungr of sóit

'Tis time to speak from the Sage's Seat;
hard by the Well of Weird I saw and was silent,
I saw and pondered,
I listened to the speech of men.

110.   I will sing from the Sage's chair
by the sacred spring of the Norns,
I looked, listened, and thought of the words of the wise,
they talked of runes and what they reveal
at the High one's hall, this is what I heard:

Baugeið Óðinn
hygg ek at unnit hafi
hvat skal hans tryggðum trúa?
Suttung svikinn
hann lét sumbli frá
ok grœtta Gunnlöðu

Of runes they spoke, and the reading of runes
was little withheld from their lips:
at the High One's hall, in the High One's hall,
I thus heard the High One say:

---

111.   Take warning to my words, Loddfafnir,
you will do best to believe me,
follow the advice I give, and you will do well,
do not get up after dark except to guard your house,
go outside only to relieve yourself.

Mál er at þylja
þular stóli á
Urðar brunni at
sá ek ok þagðak
sá ek ok hugðak
hlýdda ek á manna mál
of rúnar heyrða ek dœma
né um ráðum þögþu
Háva höllu at
Háva höllu í
heyrða ek segja svá

I counsel thee, Stray-Singer,
accept my counsels,
they will be thy boon if thou obey'st them,
they will work thy weal if thou win'st them:
rise never at nighttime,
except thou art spying or seekest a spot without.

112. Take warning to my words, Loddfafnir,
you will do best to believe me,
follow the advice I give,
and you will do well,
never lie to a volva for love,
for she may lock your arms to hers;

Ráðumk þér Loddfáfnir
en þú ráð nemir
njóta mundu ef þú nemr
þér munu góð ef þú getr
nótt þú rísat
nema á njósn sér
eða þú leitir þér innan út staðar

I counsel thee, Stray-Singer, accept my counsels,
they will be thy boon if thou obey'st them,
they will work thy weal if thou win'st them:
thou shalt never sleep in the arms of a sorceress,
lest she should lock thy limbs;

---

113. She will cast a spell so that you
will not want to be among men any longer,
rejecting meat and all sports,
you will seek your bed in sadness.

Ráðumk þér Loddfáfnir
en þú ráð nemir
njóta mundu ef þú nemr
þér munu góð ef þú getr
fjölkunnigri konu
skalattu í faðmi sofa
svá at hon lyki þik liðum

So shall she charm that thou shalt
not heed the council, or words of the king,
nor care for thy food, or the joys of mankind,
but fall into sorrowful sleep.

---

114. Take warning to my words, Loddfafnir,
you will do best to believe me,
follow the advice I give,
never take another man's wife into your bed.

Hon svá gørir
at þú gáir eigi
þings né þjóðans máls
mat þú villat
né mannskis gaman
ferr þú sorgafullr at sofa

I counsel thee, Stray-Singer, accept my counsels,
they will be thy boon if thou obey'st them,
they will work thy weal if thou win'st them:
seek not ever to draw to thyself
in love-whispering another's wife.

115. Take warning to my words, Loddfafnir,
you will do best to believe me,
follow the advice I give,
if you want to travel far and wide,
do not forget to take food.

Ráðumk þér Loddfáfnir
en þú ráð nemir
njóta mundu ef þú nemr
þér munu góð ef þú getr
annars konu
teygðu þér aldregi
eyrarúnu at

I counsel thee, Stray-Singer,
accept my counsels,
they will be thy boon if thou obey'st them,
they will work thy weal if thou win'st them:
should thou long to fare over
fell and firth provide thee well with food.

116. Take warning to my words, Loddfafnir,
you will do best to believe me,
follow the advice I give,
never tell a foe you lost your luck,
you will be ill rewarded if you trust them

Ráðumk þér Loddfáfnir
en þú ráð nemir
njóta mundu ef þú nemr
þér munu góð ef þú getr
á fjalli eða firði
ef þik fara tíðir
fásktu at virði vel

I counsel thee, Stray-Singer, accept my counsels,
they will be thy boon if thou obey'st them,
they will work thy weal if thou win'st them:
tell not ever an evil man
if misfortunes thee befall,
from such ill friend thou needst
never seek return
for thy trustful mind.

117.

I saw a man stabbed deeper than
any by a woman's mere words,
her words were death to him,
all she said was a lie.

Ráðumk þér Loddfáfnir
en þú ráð nemir
njóta mundu ef þú nemr
þér munu góð ef þú getr
illan mann
láttu aldregi
óhöpp at þér vita
því at af illum manni
fær þú aldregi
gjöld ins góða hugar

Wounded to death, have I seen a man
by the words of an evil woman;
a lying tongue had bereft him of life,
and all without reason of right.

118.

Take warning to my words, Loddfafnir,
you will do best to believe me,
follow the advice I give,
if you have true faith in a friend visit him often,
for the path not traveled is over grown quickly.

Ofarla bíta
ek sá einum hal
orð illrar konu;
fláráð tunga
varð honum at fjörlagi
ok þeygi um sanna sök

I counsel thee, Stray-Singer, accept my counsels,
they will be thy boon if thou obey'st them,
they will work thy weal if thou win'st them:
hast thou a friend whom thou trustest well,
fare thou to find him oft;
for with brushwood grows
and with grasses high
the path where no foot doth pass.

119.   Take warning to my words, Loddfafnir,
you will do best to believe me,
follow the advice I give,
rejoice in talk with a trusted friend,
and learn many healing spells
throughout your life.

Ráðumk þér Loddfáfnir
en þú ráð nemir
njóta mundu ef þú nemr
þér munu góð ef þú getr
veiztu ef þú vin átt
þanns þú vel trúir
farðu at finna opt
því at hrísi vex
ok hávu grasi
vegr er vættki trøðr

I counsel thee, Stray-Singer, accept my counsels,
they will be thy boon if thou obey'st them,
they will work thy weal if thou win'st them:
in sweet converse call the righteous to thy side,
learn a healing song while thou livest.

---

120.   Take warning to my words, Loddfafnir,
you will do best to believe me,
follow the advice I give,
always be faithful,
never be the one to fail a friendship,
sadness takes over the heart
that must conceal itself.

Ráðumk þér Loddfáfnir
en þú ráð nemir
njóta mundu ef þú nemr
þér munu góð ef þú getr
góðan mann
teygðu þér at gamanrúnum
ok nem líknargaldr meðan þú lifir

I counsel thee, Stray-Singer, accept my counsels,
they will be thy boon if thou obey'st them,
they will work thy weal if thou win'st them:
be never the first with friend of thine
to break the bond of fellowship;
care shall gnaw thy heart
if thou canst not tell all thy mind to another.

121.

Take warning to my words, Loddfafnir,
you will do best to believe me,
follow the advice I give,
if you are smart you will not exchange
words with fools along your path.

Ráðumk þér Loddfáfnir
en þú ráð nemir
njóta mundu ef þú nemr
þér munu góð ef þú getr
vin þínum
ver þú aldregi
fyrri at flaumslitum
sorg etr hjarta
ef þú segja ne náir
einhverjum allan hug

I counsel thee, Stray-Singer, accept my counsels,
they will be thy boon if thou obey'st them,
they will work thy weal if thou win'st them:
never in speech with a foolish knave
shouldst thou waste a single word.

122.

If a person is not good
they will never give you a rightful reward,
a worthwhile man will help you
on your journey to win favor and fame.

Ráðumk þér Loddfáfnir
en þú ráð nemir
njóta mundu ef þú nemr
þér munu góð ef þú getr
orðum skipta
þú skalt aldregi
við ósvinna apa

From the lips of such thou needst not look
for reward of thine own good will;
but a righteous man by praise
will render thee firm in favour and love.

123.

True bonds are formed when
men keep true to their friendship.
Anything is better than a breach in trust,
a true friend will tell you what you need to hear
instead of what you want to hear.

því at af illum manni
mundu aldregi
góðs laun um geta
en góðr maðr
mun þik gørva mega
líknfastan at lofi

There is mingling in friendship
when man can utter all his whole mind to another;
there is nought so vile as a fickle tongue;
no friend is he who but flatters.

124. Take warning to my words, Loddfafnir,
you will do best to believe me,
follow the advice I give,
do not offer words to a foe,
good men come to grief
when the bad make wars.

Sifjum er þá blandat
hverr er segja ræðr
einum allan hug
alt er betra
en sé brigðum at vera
era sá vinr öðrum
er vilt eitt segir

I counsel thee, Stray-Singer, accept my counsels,
they will be thy boon if thou obey'st them,
they will work thy weal if thou win'st them:
oft the worst lays the best one low.

---

125. Take warning to my words, Loddfafnir,
you will do best to believe me,
follow the advice I give,
only make shoes and
spear shafts you are going to use,
ill fitted shoes or a crooked spear
will lead to bad luck.

Ráðumk þér Loddfáfnir
en þú ráð nemir
njóta mundu ef þú nemr
þér munu góð ef þú getr
þrimr orðum senna
skalattu þér við verra mann
opt inn betri bilar
þá er inn verri vegr

I counsel thee, Stray-Singer, accept my counsels,
they will be thy boon if thou obey'st them,
they will work thy weal if thou win'st them:
be not a shoemaker nor yet a shaft maker
save for thyself alone:
let the shoe be misshapen, or crooked the shaft,
and a curse on thy head will be called.

126. Take warning to my words, Loddfafnir,
you will do best to believe me,
follow the advice I give,
when evil comes to you,
do not keep quiet
or let your enemy find peace.

Ráðumk þér Loddfáfnir
en þú ráð nemir
njóta mundu ef þú nemr
þér munu góð ef þú getr
skósmiðr þú verir
né skeptismiðr
nema þú sjálfum þér sér
skór er skapaðr illa
eða skapt sé rangt
þá er þér böls beðit

I counsel thee, Stray-Singer, accept my counsels,
they will be thy boon if thou obey'st them,
they will work thy weal if thou win'st them:
when in peril thou seest thee,
confess thee in peril,
nor ever give peace to thy foes.

---

127. Take warning to my words, Loddfafnir,
you will do best to believe me,
follow the advice I give,
do not rejoice in evil doings,
be happy to do good things

Ráðumk þér Loddfáfnir
en þú ráð nemir
njóta mundu ef þú nemr
þér munu góð ef þú getr
hvars þú böl kannt
kveðu þat bölvi at
ok gefat þínum fjándum frið

I counsel thee, Stray-Singer, accept my counsels,
they will be thy boon if thou obey'st them,
hey will work thy weal if thou win'st them:
rejoice not ever at tidings of ill,
but glad let thy soul be in good.

128. Take warning to my words, Loddfafnir,
you will do best to believe me,
follow the advice I give,
never look to the sky when in battle,
where many go mad due to fear,
an evil spell may be placed on you.

Ráðumk þér Loddfáfnir
en þú ráð nemir
njóta mundu ef þú nemr
þér munu góð ef þú getr
illu feginn
verðu aldregi
en lát þér at góðu getit

I counsel thee, Stray-Singer, accept my counsels,
they will be thy boon if thou obey'st them,
they will work thy weal if thou win'st them:
look not up in battle,
when men are as beasts,
lest the wights bewitch thee with spells.

---

129. Take warning to my words, Loddfafnir,
you will do best to believe me,
follow the advice I give,
if you want to win a woman's love,
make good promises and keep them,
no one tires of the treasure they get.

Ráðumk þér Loddfáfnir
en þú ráð nemir
njóta mundu ef þú nemr
þér munu góð ef þú getr
upp líta
skalattu í orrostu
gjalti glíkir
verða gumna synir
síðr þitt um heilli halir

I counsel thee, Stray-Singer, accept my counsels,
they will be thy boon if thou obey'st them,
they will work thy weal if thou win'st them:
wouldst thou win joy of a gentle maiden,
and lure to whispering of love,
thou shalt make fair promise, and let it be fast,
none will scorn their weal who can win it.

130.

Take warning to my words, Loddfafnir,
you will do best to believe me,
follow the advice I give,
I say to you be careful,
and do not over do it,
watch out for the mead
or another man's wife,
and do not be tricked by thieves.

Ráðumk þér Loddfáfnir
en þú ráð nemir
njóta mundu ef þú nemr
þér munu góð ef þú getr
ef þú vilt þér góða konu
kveðja at gamanrúnum
ok fá fögnuð af
fögru skaltu heita
ok láta fast vera
leiðisk manngi gott ef getr

I counsel thee, Stray-Singer, accept my counsels,
they will be thy boon if thou obey'st them,
they will work thy weal if thou win'st them:
I pray thee be wary, yet not too wary,
be wariest of all with ale, with another's wife,
and a third thing eke,
that knaves outwit thee never.

131.

Take warning to my words, Loddfafnir,
you will do best to believe me,
follow the advice I give,
never mock your guests,
or make fun of a man
you may meet on your path.

Ráðumk þér Loddfáfnir
en þú ráð nemir
njóta mundu ef þú nemr
þér munu góð ef þú getr
varan bið ek þik vera
en eigi ofvaran
ver þú við öl varastr
ok við annars konu
ok við þat it þriðja
at þjófar ne leiki

I counsel thee, Stray-Singer, accept my counsels,
they will be thy boon if thou obey'st them,
they will work thy weal if thou win'st them:
hold not in scorn,
nor mock in thy halls
a guest or wandering wight.

132. Those already there,
often cannot tell a new person's kin.
You will never find someone without faults,
or one completely evil and has no use.

Ráðumk þér Loddfáfnir
en þú ráð nemir
njóta mundu ef þú nemr
þér munu góð ef þú getr
at háði né hlátri
hafðu aldregi
gest né ganganda

They know but unsurely who sit within
what manner of man is come: none is
found so good, but some fault attends him,
or so ill but he serves for somewhat.

---

133. Take warning to my words, Loddfafnir,
you will do best to believe me,
follow the advice I give,
never make fun of long-bearded sages.
You will learn a lot listening to the elders.

Opt vitu ógörla
þeir er sitja inni fyrir
hvers þeir ro kyns er koma
erat maðr svá góðr
at galli ne fylgi
né svá illr at einugi dugi

I counsel thee, Stray-Singer,
accept my counsels,
they will be thy boon if thou obey'st them,
they will work thy weal if thou win'st them:
hold never in scorn the hoary singer;
oft the counsel of the old is good;
come words of wisdom
from the withered lips of him
left to hang among hides,
to rock with the rennets
and swing with the skins.

134. Take warning to my words, Loddfafnir,
you will do best to believe me,
follow the advice I give,
do not brush off a guest or show them to the gate,
be good to the poor.

*Ráðumk þér Loddfáfnir
en þú ráð nemir
njóta mundu ef þú nemr
þér munu góð ef þú getr
at hárum þul
hlæðu aldregi
opt er gott þat er gamlir kveða
opt ór skörpum belg
skilin orð koma
þeim er hangir með hám
ok skollir með skrám
ok váfir með vílmögum*

*I counsel thee, Stray-Singer, accept my counsels,
they will be thy boon if thou obey'st them,
they will work thy weal if thou win'st them:
growl not at guests,
nor drive them from the gate
but show thyself gentle to the poor.*

---

135. The door must be closed with a heavy beam
which opens for new guest,
make sure to lock it with a ring
or you will receive anger as a reward.

*Ráðumk þér Loddfáfnir
en þú ráð nemir
njóta mundu ef þú nemr
þér munu góð ef þú getr
gest þú ne geyja
né á grind hrekir
get þú váluðum vel*

*Mighty is the bar to be moved away
for the entering in of all.
Shower thy wealth,
or men shall wish thee every ill in thy limbs.*

136.

Take warning to my words, Loddfafnir,
you will do best to believe me,
follow the advice I give,
the earth may help if you are drinking mead,
the earth fights mead, fire fights off sickness,
acorns if you have constipation,
corn works against witchcraft,
the moon soothes hate,
alum for sick cattle,
runes for any misfortune.
Great floods will end the world.

Rammt er þat tré
er ríða skal
öllum at upploki
baug þú gef
eða þat biðja mun
þér læs hvers á liðu

I counsel thee, Stray-Singer, accept my counsels,
they will be thy boon if thou obey'st them,
they will work thy weal if thou win'st them:
when ale thou quaffest, call upon earth's might,
'tis earth drinks in the floods.
Earth prevails o'er drink, but fire o'er sickness,
the oak o'er binding,
the earcorn o'er witchcraft,
the rye spur o'er rupture,
he moon o'er rages, herb o'er cattle plagues,
runes o'er harm.

137.

Odin said:
I know I hung from a high tree for nine nights,
pierced by a spear; Odin's pledge given myself to myself.
No one can tell of the tree from its deep roots.

Ráðumk þér Loddfáfnir
en þú ráð nemir
njóta mundu ef þú nemr
þér munu góð ef þú getr
hvars þú öl drekkr
kjós þú þér jarðar megin
því at jörð tekr við öldri
en eldr við sóttum
eik við abbindi
ax við fjölkynngi
höll við hýrógi
heiptum skal mána kveðja
beiti við bitsóttum
en við bölvi rúnar
fold skal við flóð taka

I trow I hung on that windy Tree
nine whole days and nights,
stabbed with a spear, offered to Odin,
myself to mine own self given,
high on that Tree of which none hath heard from
what roots it rises to heaven.

138.   I was brought no bread or mead,
I looked toward the ground,
crying out loud, I caught up runes,
I then finally fell to the ground.

Veit ek at ek hekk
vindga meiði á   None refreshed me ever with food or drink,
nætr allar níu   I peered right down in the deep;
geiri undaðr   crying aloud I lifted the Runes
ok gefinn Óðni   then back I fell from thence.
sjálfr sjálfum mér
á þeim meiði
er manngi veit
hvers hann af rótum renn

---

139.   Nine great songs I learned
from the son of Bolthorn,
and I drank of the costly mead
the holy vessel held.

Við hleifi mik sældu   Nine mighty songs
né við hornigi   I learned from the great son of Bale-thorn,
nýsta ek niðr   Bestla's sire;
nam ek upp rúnar   I drank a measure of the wondrous Mead,
œpandi nam   with the Soulstirrer's drops I was showered.
fell ek aptr þaðan

---

140.   I learned the lore, thriving with wisdom,
I learned words from the words I sought after,
verses multiplied from verses I sought out.

Fimbulljóð níu   Ere long I bare fruit, and throve full well,
nam ek af inum frægja syni   I grew and waxed in wisdom;
Bölþórs Bestlu föður   word following word, I found me words,
ok ek drykk of gat   deed following deed, I wrought deeds.
ins dýra mjaðar
ausinn Óðreri

141.
You will find runes and read the staves,
strong magic and spells,
set down by the Sage,
that the gods made,
the wisdom of Odin.

Þá nam ek frævask
ok fróðr vera
ok vaxa ok vel hafask
orð mér af orði
orðs leitaði
verk mér af verki
verks leitaði

Hidden Runes shalt thou seek and interpreted signs,
many symbols of might and power,
by the great Singer painted,
by the high Powers fashioned,
graved by the Utterer of gods.

142.
Odin for the Aesir,
Dain for the elf,
Dvalin for the dwarfs,
Asvid for the giants,
some I made myself.

Rúnar munt þú finna
ok ráðna stafi
mjök stóra stafi
mjök stinna stafi
er fáði fimbulþulr
ok gørðu ginnregin
ok reist Hroptr rögna

For gods graved Odin,
for elves graved Daïn,
Dvalin the Dallier for dwarfs,
All-wise for Jötuns, and I, of myself,
graved some for the sons of men.

143.
Can you write?
Can you read?
Can you paint?
Can you prove something?
Can you wish?
Can you worship?
Can you summon?
Can you do a sacrifice?

Óðinn með ásum
en fyr álfum Dáinn
ok Dvalinn dvergum fyrir
Ásviðr jötnum fyrir
ek reist sjálfr sumar

Dost know how to write, dost know how to read,
dost know how to paint, dost know how to prove,
dost know how to ask,
dost know how to offer, dost know how to send,
dost know how to spend?

144.

It is better to have no prayers
than to have too many gifts,
gifts only look for other gifts,
better to be forgotten than over fed.
This is what Odin wrote before the world began,
where he rose up and returned.

Veiztu hvé rísta skal?
Veiztu hvé ráða skal?
Veiztu hvé fá skal?
Veiztu hvé freista skal?
Veiztu hvé biðja skal?
Veiztu hvé blóta skal?
Veiztu hvé senda skal?
Veiztu hvé sóa skal?

Better ask for too little than offer too much,
like the gift should be the boon;
better not to send than to overspend.
Thus Odin graved ere the world began;
Then he rose from the deep, and came again.

145.

I know a spell:
no king's wife can speak,
and no man has ever mastered,
and is called "Help" for it can comfort
the sick and cast out all sorrows.

Betra er óbeðit
en sé ofblótit
ey sér til gildis gjöf
betra er ósent
en sé ofsóit
svá Þundr um reist
fyr þjóða rök
þar hann upp um reis
er hann aptr of kom

Those songs I know,
which nor sons of men nor queen
in a king's court knows;
the first is Help which will bring thee help
in all woes and in sorrow and strife.

146.

I know another:
that men need if they
want to be true healers.

Ljóð ek þau kann
er kannat þjóðans kona
ok mannskis mögr
hjálp heitir eitt
en þat þér hjálpa mun
við sökum ok sorgum
ok sútum görvöllum

A second I know,
which the son of men must sing,
who would heal the sick.

147.

I know a third:
if needed that defeats any foe,
it blunts their sword,
their will and weapons will fail against me.

Þat kann ek annat
er þurfu ýta synir
þeir er vilja læknar lifa

A third I know: if sore need should come
of a spell to stay my foes;
when I sing that song,
which shall blunt their swords,
nor their weapons nor staves can wound.

148.

I know a fourth:
if I should be fettered,
I shout it and it sets me free
and breaks my bonds of hand and foot.

Þat kann ek it þriðja
ef mér verðr þörf mikil
hapts við mína heiptmögu
eggjar ek deyfi
minna andskota
bítat þeim vápn né velir

A fourth I know: if men make fast
in chains the joints of my limbs,
when I sing that song which shall set me free,
spring the fetters from hands and feet.

149.

I know a fifth:
for battle's fury,
if someone throws a spear,
it travels slow so that I can stop it,
all I have to do is see it.

Þat kann ek it fjórða
ef mér fyrðar bera
bönd at bóglimum
svá ek gel
at ek ganga má
sprettr mér af fótum fjöturr
en af höndum hapt

A fifth I know:
when I see, by foes shot,
speeding a shaft through the host,
flies it never so strongly I still can stay it,
if I get but a glimpse of its flight.

150.

I know a sixth:
if someone would try to harm me
by writing runes against me
on a tree root the harm will come
to the other person, not me.

Þat kann ek it fimmta
ef ek sé af fári skotinn
flein í fólki vaða
flýgra hann svá stinnt
at ek stöðvigak
ef ek hann sjónum of sék

A sixth I know:
when some thane would harm me
in runes on a moist tree's root,
on his head alone shall light the ills
of the curse that he called upon mine.

151.

I know a seventh:
if I see flames rising high around a hall,
no matter how high they get
my spell will stop them.

Þat kann ek it sétta
ef mik særir þegn
á rótum rams viðar
ok þann hal
er mik heipta kveðr
þann eta mein heldr en mik

A seventh I know:
if I see a hall
high o'er the bench-mates blazing,
flame it ne'er so fiercely I still can save it,
I know how to sing that song.

152.

I know an eighth:
which no one on earth could not find useful.
When hate rises between warriors
the spell will sooth them.

Þat kann ek it sjaunda
ef ek sé hávan loga
sal um sessmögum
brennrat svá breitt
at ek honum bjargigak
þann kann ek galdr at gala

An eighth I know:
which all can sing
for their weal if they learn it well;
where hate shall wax 'mid the warrior sons,
I can calm it soon with that song.

153.

I know a ninth:
If I ever need to save my ship from a storm at sea,
it will calm the wind and waves.

Þat kann ek it átta
er öllum er
nytsamligt at nema
hvars hatr vex
með hildings sonum
þat má ek bœta brátt

A ninth I know:
when need befalls me
to save my vessel afloat, I hush the wind
on the stormy wave, and soothe all the sea to rest.

154.

I know a tenth:
if at any time I see volvas in the sky,
the spell when sung will send them off their course,
once they lose their wits,
they cannot return home.

Þat kann ek it níunda
ef mik nauðr um stendr
at bjarga fari mínu á floti
vind ek kyrri
vági á
ok svæfik allan sæ

A tenth I know:
when at night the witches ride
and sport in the air,
such spells I weave that they wander home
out of skins and wits bewildered.

155.

I know an eleventh:
if I lead friends to war,
under my shield I shout the spell,
and it makes them faster,
they fare well in the fight,
they also fare well coming from the fight,
and will fare well wherever they go.

Þat kann ek it tíunda
ef ek sé túnriðir
leika lopti á
ek svá vinnk
at þeir villir fara
sinna heimhama
sinna heimhuga

An eleventh I know:
if haply I lead
my old comrades out to war,
I sing 'neath the shields, and they fare
forth mightily safe into battle,
safe out of battle, and safe return
from the strife.

156.

I know a twelfth:
if I see a dead man hanging in a tree,
the mighty runes I write will make them
come down and speak with me.

Þat kann ek it ellipta
ef ek skal til orrostu
leiða langvini
undir randir ek gel
en þeir með ríki fara
heilir hildar til
heilir hildi frá
koma þeir heilir hvaðan

A twelfth I know:
if I see in a tree
a corpse from a halter hanging,
such spells I write, and paint in runes,
that the being descends and speaks.

157.

I know a thirteenth:
if I pour water over a youth,
they will not fall in a fight and
no sword can kill them.

Þat kann ek it tólpta
ef ek sé á tré uppi
váfa virgilná
svá ek ríst
ok í rúnum fák
at sá gengr gumi
ok mælir við mik

A thirteenth I know:
if the new-born son
of a warrior I sprinkle with water,
that youth will not fail when he fares to war,
never slain shall he bow before sword.

158.

I know a fourteenth:
as men will find out,
when I tell tales of the gods:
I know about them all,
few can say as much.

Þat kann ek it þrettánda
ef ek skal þegn ungan
verpa vatni á
munat hann falla
þótt hann í fólk komi
hnígra sá halr fyr hjörum

A fourteenth I know:
if I needs must number the Powers
to the people of men,
I know all the nature of gods and of elves
which none can know untaught.

159.

I know a fifteenth:
what Thjodrorir chanted at Delling's door,
power to the Aesir, victory to the elves,
understanding given to Odin.

Þat kann ek it fjórtánda
ef ek skal fyrða liði
telja tíva fyrir
ása ok álfa
ek kann allra skil
fár kann ósnotr svá

A fifteenth I know,
which Folk-stirrer sang, the dwarf,
at the gates of Dawn;
he sang strength to the gods,
and skill to the elves,
and wisdom to Odin who utters.

160.

I know a sixteenth:
if I say that spell,
any woman grants me my desires,
I win the heart of the maiden
and turn her thought where I want.

Þat kann ek it fimmtánda
er gól Þjóðreyrir
dvergr fyr Dellings durum
afl gól hann ásum
en álfum frama
hyggju Hroptatý

A sixteenth I know:
when all sweetness and love
I would win from some artful wench,
her heart I turn,
and the whole mind change
of that fair-armed lady I love.

161.   I know a seventeenth:
with it, no maiden can forsake me.

Þat kann ek it sextánda
ef ek vil ins svinna mans
hafa geð alt ok gaman
hugi ek hverfi
hvítarmri konu
ok sný ek hennar öllum sefa

A seventeenth I know:
so that e'en
the shy maiden is slow to shun my love.

---

162.   But all this, Loddfafnir,
you will lack,
though it would do you good to have it,
and it would be needed if you knew it.

Þat kann ek it sjautjánda
at mik mun seint firrask
it manunga man
ljóða þessa
mun þú Loddfáfnir
lengi vanr vera
þó sé þér góð ef þú getr
nýt ef þú nemr
þörf ef þú þiggr

These songs, Stray-Singer,
which man's son knows not,
long shalt thou lack in life,
though thy weal if thou win'st them,
thy boon if thou obey'st them thy good
if haply thou gain'st them.

---

163.   I know an eighteenth:
that I never tell,
to maiden or wife of man,
a secret I hide from all
except the love who lies in my arms,
or else my own sister.

Þat kann ek it átjánda
er ek æva kennik
mey né manns konu
alt er betra
er einn um kann
þat fylgir ljóða lokum
nema þeiri einni
er mik armi verr
eða mín systir sé

An eighteenth I know:
which I ne'er shall tell to maiden or wife of man
save alone to my sister, or haply to her
who folds me fast in her arms;
most safe are secrets known to but one-
the songs are sung to an end.

164.
The sayings of the High One are
helpful to men and their sons,
and harmful to the giants.
Hail to the speaker and the one taught!
They are lucky to have the lore,
and happy if they are in need of it.

Nú era Háva mál　　　　　　　　*Now the sayings of the High One*
kveðin Háva höllu í　　　　*are uttered in the hall for the weal of men,*
allþörf ýta sonum　　　　　　*for the woe of Jötuns. Hail,*
óþörf jötna sonum　　　　　　*thou who hast spoken!*
heill sá er kvað　　　　　　　*Hail, thou that knowest!*
heill sá er kann　　　　　　　*Hail, ye that have hearkened!*
njóti sá er nam　　　　　　　*Use, thou who hast learned!*
heilir þeirs hlýddu

NOTES

NOTES

NOTES

CPSIA information can be obtained
at www.ICGtesting.com
Printed in the USA
FSHW021607150320
68008FS